Little Skill Seekers

HANDWRITING PRACTICE

MSCHOLASTIC

New York • Toronto • London • Auckland • Sydney • New Delhi
Mexico City • Hong Kong • Buenos Aires

Cover Design: Tannaz Fassihi
Cover Illustration: Michael Robertson
Interior Design: Mina Chen
Interior Illustration: Doug Jones

Scholastic Inc., 557 Broadway, New York, NY 10012
ISBN: 978-1-338-30637-8
Copyright © Scholastic Inc. All rights reserved. Printed in the U.S.A.
First printing, March 2019.

3 4 5 6 7 8 9 10   40   24 23 22 21

Dear Parent,

Welcome to *Little Skill Seekers: Handwriting Practice*! Fine-motor skills practice leads to clear, legible handwriting—this workbook will help your child develop this ability.

Help your little skill seeker build a strong foundation for learning by choosing more books in the Little Skill Seekers series. The exciting and colorful workbooks in the series are designed to set your child on the path to success. Each book targets essential skills important to your child's development.

Here are some key features of *Little Skill Seekers: Handwriting Practice* and the other workbooks in this series:

- Filled with colorful illustrations that make learning fun and playful

- Provides plenty of opportunity to practice essential skills

- Builds independence as children work through the pages on their own, at their own pace

- Comes in a perfect size that fits easily in a backpack for practice on the go

Now let's get started on this journey to help your child become a successful, lifelong learner!

—The Editors

A a

Trace and write.

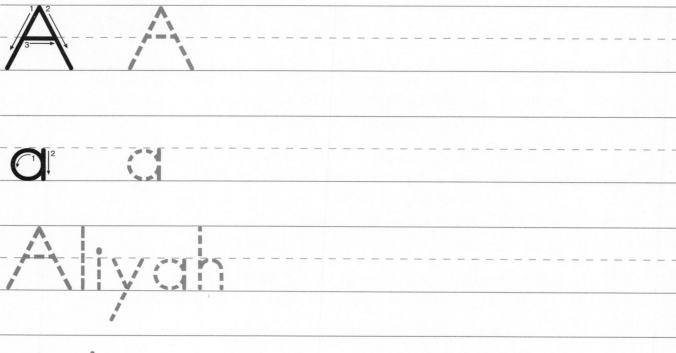

A A

a a

Aliyah

ants

Trace and write the sentence.

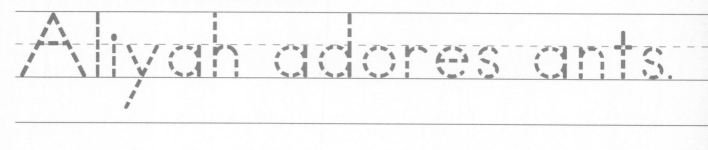

Aliyah adores ants.

B b

Trace and write.

B B

b b

Bert

bears

Trace and write the sentence.

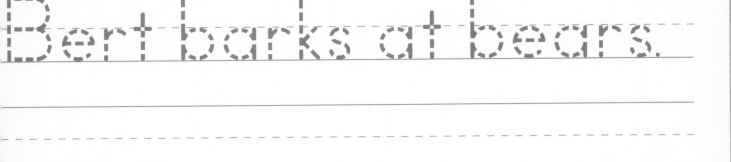

Bert barks at bears.

Cc

Trace and write.

C C

c c

Carla

cats

Trace and write the sentence.

Carla cares for cats.

Dd

Trace and write.

D D

d d

Diego

dogs

Trace and write the sentence.

Diego draws dogs.

E e

Trace and write.

Trace and write the sentence.

8

Ff

Trace and write.

F F

f f

Felix

frogs

Trace and write the sentence.

Felix feeds frogs.

Gg

Trace and write.

G   G

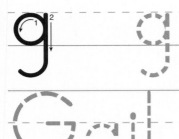

g   g

Gail

goats

Trace and write the sentence.

Gail grins at goats.

Hh

Trace and write.

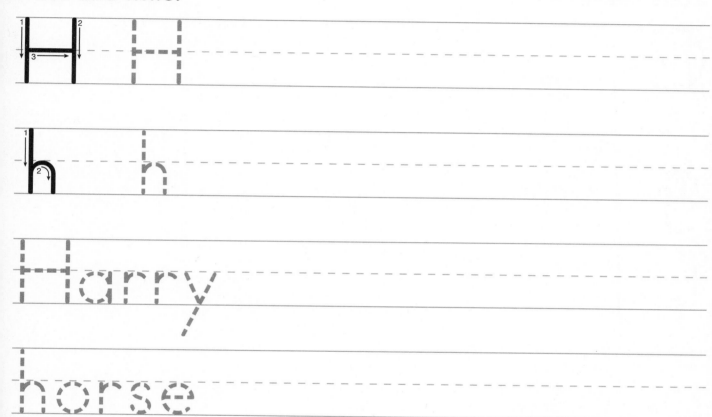

H H H

h h

Harry

horse

Trace and write the sentence.

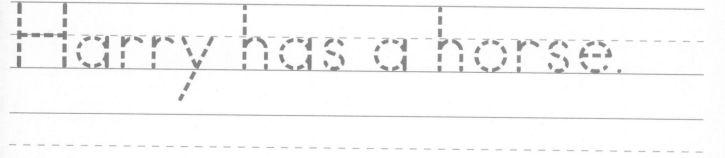

Harry has a horse.

I i

Trace and write.

I   I

i   i

Iris

iguana

Trace and write the sentence.

Iris is an iguana.

Jj

Trace and write.

J　J　J

j　j　j

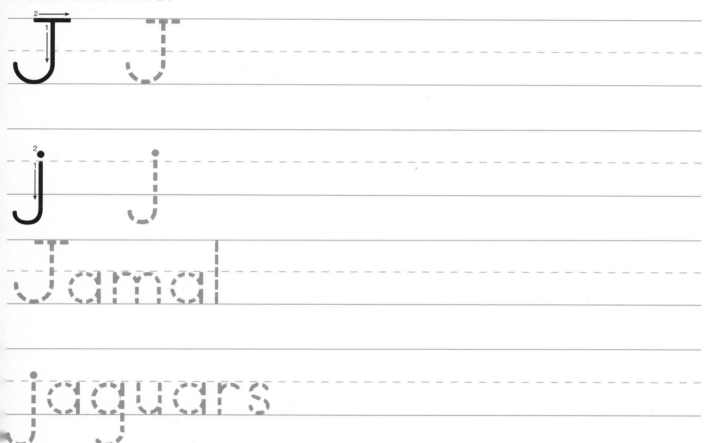

Jamal

jaguars

Trace and write the sentence.

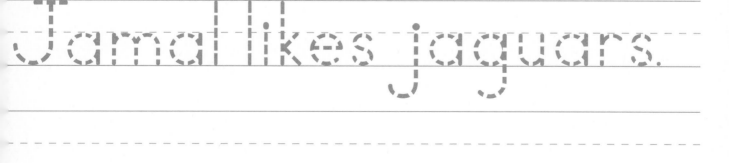

Jamal likes jaguars.

Kk

Trace and write.

K K

k k

Kiara

koala

Trace and write the sentence.

Kiara is a koala.

Ll

Trace and write.

L   L

l   l

Logan

lions

Trace and write the sentence.

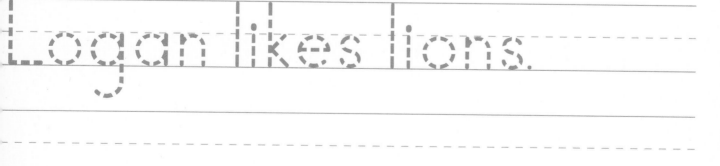

Logan likes lions.

Mm

Trace and write.

M M M

m m

Mia

monkey

Trace and write the sentence.

Mia meets a monkey.

Nn

Trace and write.

N   N   N

n   n

Neil

newts

Trace and write the sentence.

Neil likes newts.

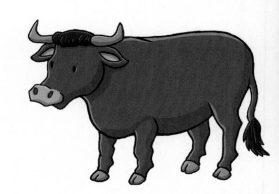

Trace and write.

O

o

Olga

oxen

Trace and write the sentence.

Olga owns oxen.

Pp

Trace and write.

P   P   P

p   p   p

Pablo

parrot

Trace and write the sentence.

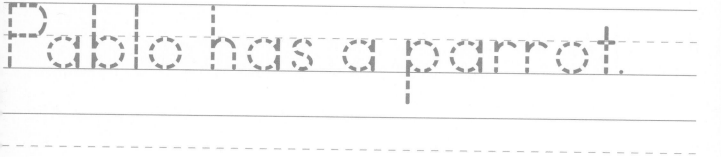

Pablo has a parrot.

Qq

Trace and write.

Q   Q

q   q

Quisha

quail

Trace and write the sentence.

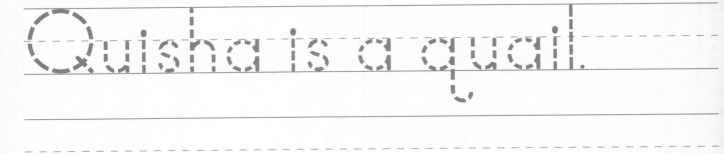

Quisha is a quail.

R r

Trace and write.

R R R

r r r

Raul

rabbits

Trace and write the sentence.

Raul raises rabbits.

Ss

Trace and write.

 S

 s

sheep

Trace and write the sentence.

T t

Trace and write.

T   T

t   t

Tom

tigers

Trace and write the sentence.

Tom likes tigers.

U u

Trace and write.

U U

u u

Umi

unicorns

Trace and write the sentence.

Umi likes unicorns.

V v

Trace and write.

V V V

V v v

Vance

vulture

Trace and write the sentence.

Vance saw a vulture.

Ww

Trace and write.

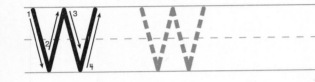

 w

 Wilda

 whale

Trace and write the sentence.

 Wilda saw a whale.

Trace and write.

X   X

x   x

Xeno

x-ray fish

Trace and write the sentence.

Xeno is an x-ray fish.

Yy

Trace and write.

Y   Y

y   y

Yara

yaks

Trace and write the sentence.

Yara yaps at yaks.

Zz

Trace and write.

Z Z

z z

Zane

zebra

Trace and write the sentence.

Zane is a zebra.

Numbers 1–10

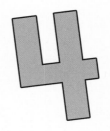

1 2 3 4 5

Trace and write.

6 7 8 9 10

Trace and write.

6

7

8

9

10

Color Words

Trace and write.

red

yellow

blue

green

orange

Trace and write.

purple

pink

white

brown

black

Number Words

Trace and write.

one

two

three

four

five

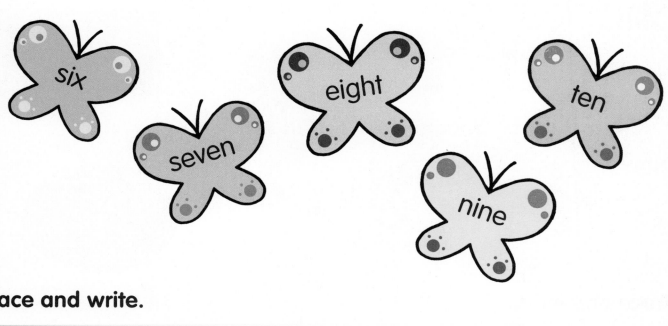

Trace and write.

six

seven

eight

nine

ten

Shapes

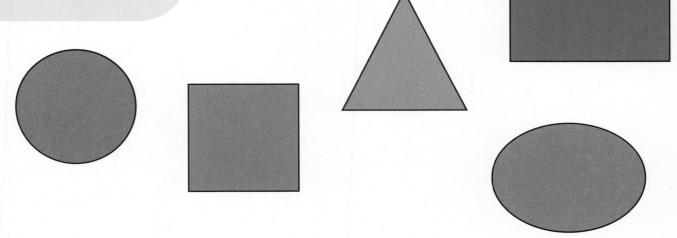

Trace and write.

circle

square

triangle

rectangle

oval

Trace and write.

diamond

star

heart

pentagon

octagon

Seasons

Trace and write.

spring

summer

fall

winter

Days of the Week

Trace and write.

Monday

Tuesday

Wednesday

Thursday

Friday

Saturday

Sunday

Months of the Year

Trace and write.

January

February

March

April

May

June

Trace and write.

July

August

September

October

November

December

Farm Animals

Trace and write.

cow

dog

donkey

duck

goose

goat

Trace and write.

hen

horse

pig

rooster

sheep

turkey

Action Words

Trace and write.

cook

eat

walk

drink

read

sleep

Trace and write.

talk

dance

write

run

play

sing

Describing Words

Trace and write.

salty

sweet

sour

spicy

hot

cold

Trace and write.

big

small

tall

pretty

soft

sharp

Describing Words

Trace and write.

loud

hard

dirty

wet

open

closed